ll Dress One Night As You

RISSIE GITTINS was born in Lancashire and lives in South
ndon. She studied at Newcastle University and St Martin's
hool of Art. Her poems have been anthologized, broadcast on
C Radio 4 and animated for Cbeebies television. Two of her
ildren's poems won Belmont Poetry Prizes in 2002 and her first
llection of children's poems *Now You See Me, Now You ...* (Rabbit
ole, 2002) was shortlisted for the inaugural CLPE Poetry Award
1 2003. Her first adult poetry collection *Armature* was published
y Arc in 2003. Her second children's poetry collection *I Don't
Vant an Avocado for an Uncle* (Rabbit Hole, 2006) was shortlisted for
he CLPE Poetry Award 2007 and was a Poetry Book Society
hoice for the Children's Poetry Bookshelf.

1 2007 her first book of short stories *Family Connections* appeared
om Salt. Her plays for BBC Radio 4 include *Starved for Love*, *Life
surance*, and *Dinner in the Iguanodon*. She has received a
awthornden Fellowship, an Arts Council Grant for the Arts, and
vards from the Royal Literary Fund and the Author's
undation. She is a member of the Poetry Society's Poetryclass
am.

Also by Chrissie Gittins

I'll Dress One Night As You

CHRISSIE GITTINS

SALT

CAMBRIDGE

PUBLISHED BY SALT PUBLISHING
14a High Street, Fulbourn, Cambridge CB21 5DH United Kingdom

Salt Publishing 2009

Printed and bound in the United Kingdom by MPG Books Group

Typeset in Swift 9.5 / 13

ISBN 978 1 84471 516 9 hardback

Salt Publishing Ltd gratefully acknowledges
the financial assistance of Arts Council England

1 3 5 7 9 8 6 4 2

For my dear friends and family,
and in loving memory of Mabyn

Contents

Acknowledgements

My thanks to the editors of the following publications in which some of these poems were first published: *Mslexia*, *Oxford Poetry*, *The Poetry Paper* (The Poetry Trust), *The Slab*, *The Works 4* (Macmillan), *THE SHOp* (Ireland), *Other Poetry*, *Seam*, *Envoi*, *Orbis*, *Loose Scree*, *Magma*, *Quadrant* (Australia), *Jacket* (Australia).

A number of these poems first appeared in *I Don't Want an Avocado for an Uncle* (Rabbit Hole Publications, 2006).

Special thanks to Les Murray for publishing the 'Cloth' sequence of 6 poems in Quadrant.

'Dinner in the Iguanodon Mould' was shortlisted in the 2004 Middlesex University Poetry Competition. 'The Man Who Carries A Picture of Hitler' was a runner up in the *Mslexia* Poetry Competition 2005.

I am grateful to the Authors' Foundation for a grant received in 2007 to complete this collection.

Special thanks are due to friends who advised and encouraged me with this manuscript, especially Moniza Alvi and Carys Davies.

I'll Dress One Night As You

I'll Dress One Night As You

LEAVING BRANCASTER STAITHE

The pink-footed geese flew in lazy Vs
across the January skies,
the hollering came first—
so I knew to look up.

Spread like iron filings
over a starched white tablecloth
they settled on the marsh,
      a single snow goose the eye of their storm.

That afternoon I left
for your hospital bed—a flock stood sentinel
in an empty field, their heads held down
as I drove by.

The light slowly drained
from the Lincolnshire Fens
to a fine white line on the horizon,
      and this time I knew you would die.

MOTHERING SUNDAY

Shall I send a bouquet to an empty house,
remind the kitchen of the crinkle of cellophane,
whoosh a torrent of water into a vase,
snip each stem to a sharp diagonal?

Or shall I cut a rose from the garden,
place it next to a spray of acer,
surprise your bedside table
with blooms you'd forgotten you had?

The fragrance glides towards your chair,
the cerise of the rose sings to you.
Points of the leaves reach around doors,
their new buds slowly opening.

Every Night I Stayed

The way you used to come to kiss me every night I stayed—
despite an extra journey on your walking frame.

You'd push off from the kitchen on your slippers,
head down against the wind, 'I'm going now'.

I'd get up to meet you from the sitting room,
our heads would rest together in the hall.

Then back you'd go along the straits,
weaving from side to side,

till you reached the island of your bed.
You'd lie across, beside your duvet,

lapped by waves of grateful sleep.

Out of Place

Your ornaments sit
bunched up on the windowsill,
the conch shell resting on a fluted plate,
the goose tangling with the teapot.

Your photo—
a smile from a shingle beach,
faces away. Some other shots of us
have slid right down the mantelpiece—

we are in disarray,

too close, no room to look our best.
You hated anything
out of place.

I found your negligée
with a silky camisole—kept one
and bagged the other.

I'll dress one night as you,
wear your weighty beads and bracelet,
I'll stretch my lips across my teeth,

half open my mouth,
apply red lipstick in a compact mirror—
the way you did,

then fold a tissue,
imprint my lips in carmine,
and hold it up for you to see.

Retrieving the Capodimonte

I couldn't look at you cold and dead
but I saw your clock in the shop—
glowing, and chiming the quarter hour,
proud amongst other clocks.

Your sundae set, short by one,
was placed on a bathroom cupboard.
The green glass shone
that quarter to one,
making mahogany sizzle.

I bought back the figure frying his eggs
as he sat by the side of the road—
he's back in my boot, in two plastic bags,
waiting to become à la mode.

JAR

Half my life I led with you
And could not see beyond,
Half my life is gone from me,
The half that can't be found.

Now I see you in my days,
You're there to share my deeds,
But not to touch, or kiss, or hear—

You're in the scenes that play
Inside my head which show me
What you were—the light fantastic

Of your love, which makes me spin
And dare to dip my finger
In the jar of life,
The half I'll live for you.

Helen's Daughter

There's an image of her on the wall—
a painter's hand applied her cheek,
I see her bloom, her clear grey eyes,

her still, far off smile.
Her face, as she stands by the door
in readiness for school, is in shadow.

Her eyes meet mine, her haircut's new,
she's slightly older than her painted self.
Each time I pass her image on the stairs,

still serene, her eyes averted,
I think of her inside her room—
her duvet ruffled up with sleep.

She kneels before her life—
a girl in luck, a girl in tune
with minims and with swimming pools.

Say Something To Me Of Life

Say something to me of life—
that it is not random
like a stray celandine setting seed
in the middle of a lawn,
that one pre-heartbeat babe
has just as much a chance
of growing up to skip rope
as any other.

Say something to me of death—
that it is not random,
that a child may dodge a bullet,
a woman avoid tripping
so her tender throat is not pierced
on the corner of a table.

Say something to me of life—
that death will not interrupt
at any moment like a doorbell
ringing and ringing in the middle of the day.

The Man Who Carries A Picture Of Hitler

I cut it from the album,
the black felted page sticks to the back.

Head bowed, Hitler is reading the paper—
content with his success.

My grandfather guarded him well,
told me he didn't kill Jews.

And in that off moment,
with the vase of mimosa at its best,

when leaves were new through the window,
my grandfather pointed his camera.

I drive round Birmingham
with the photo deep in my wallet,

face to face with a shot of my son.
The crown of Hitler's head brushes

the wet bottom lip of my five year old,
his face is resolute, unflinching.

The rain falls and the birds still fly.

She Gave Me Her Childhood Books
for Liz

So that now, when I remember huddling with my friend
on a cold stone wall in the playground,

we're joined by the King of Peru
who falls down a well

and comforts himself with a rhyme.
The bell sounds for lessons, we fetch up in a line.

Beside us loiters a row of ducks,
an old sailor, a knight with quiet armour.

When keys are thrown at chatty Colin
the knight shields the blow.

When Fay is given the ruler,
the sailor throws a jig.

When Barry is tied to a chair,
the ducks peck at the knots.

Through the night newts climb out of a jar
to visit my dreams,

the Lord High Coachman laughs from the window,
a half bald doll squeaks her secrets in my melting ear.

Transmission

The brick was loose, like a sore tooth,
a sack spread out on the floor caught the falling mortar,

one last tug freed it from the wall.
Mrs Jump next door had run her chapped hand along the wall.

Four bricks from the fireplace, she reckoned—
so the same on the other side.

The second and third came out like a dream.
Spot on. My mother, at six, peered through the hole.

She reached out, touched the hardboard panel,
the polished oak of its surround.

When the switch was on, how would it sound?
At five o'clock she pushed a chair against the hole,

snuggled up to Children's Hour. A smile
waltzed across her lips, her eyes were fixed

on the hearth—a pile—a three-brick wall.
Later, Mrs Jump installed herself beside her set,

for Athur Askey, Tommy Handley,
Winterbottom and Murgatroyd—

'What does your watch say?'
'Tick tick!'

She breathed in then sighed.
The smell of currant cake, oxtail soup,

steak and cowheel pie was being transmitted
from the other side.

The Grandmother I Never Knew

touches a silver vase of rosebuds
on a dark carved dresser,
her gaze steady.

She's losing patience.
The latticed window behind
opens onto fake cloud.

She wants to be polishing
her own windows,
packing her husband's chest

with brown paper, sewing
the gathers into her daughter's
shantung dress. Not

standing here, poe-faced,
posing for this
one photograph

we have of her.

Chorister, St Saviour's Church, Southwark, 1607

I aim my voice at the vaults,
my truest notes, with all
the sweetness I can muster—

balm to his buboes,
calm to his fever,
unction in his resting place.

This afternoon, across the bridge,
I must exchange my surplice
for Titania's gown.

He used to be my Oberon,
each day he stroked my cheek,
I could load my eyes into his

and let my heart speak
through his brother's words.
His lips were mink on mine.

What's left? This smell
from seventy smouldering wicks,
a rare forenoon toll,

the sight of his tomb shining
from the choir floor
for as long as I can to sing?

I'll dress in foolish columbine
and strip a songbird's wing.

Self-Portrait, Filippino Lippi, c. 1485

You're there, ahead of the exhibition,
gazing from your grazed surface,

lips parted, eyes knowing
just enough to penetrate your viewer.

I'm taken in.
As I notice your re-drawn ear
I believe in the warmth of your cheek,
the recess within your chin.

Your stasis stands as a moment
when a boy-man glances my way,

when hair, lips, lines and paint
adhere in a look,
triggering my blood to tilt.

Landscape and Portrait

There's rain enough to re-surface the sea,
waterfalls — white fissures down the hills.

I'm clouded in, my house enclosed
with muslin drifts of spray.

Another layer lies between the sky
and my gentle sitting room.

There are birds painted blue, rubbed with sand,
frogs jump from rounded bellies,

a mermaid's tears turn to stone.
Oil paint cradles a giant fish,

gives orange to a bedroom floor,
sounds a warning temple bell.

Your canvases lie and stand,
stacked and propped against your life.

I'm keeping them together,
a textured birth above my head.

You paint me, in my dreams,
bring sable brushes to our bed.

The Carpet Fitter's Wife

As I teach the isosceles triangle
to a class of disbelieving faces,
my husband offers bell twist and finepoint
to the women of Lancashire.

We mark our angles with an arc,
plot lines with protractors,
place shapes in space
in blue-squared folded notebooks.

He points to 'Windermere Lake, Vellum,
Cottonwood' for the owners
of long bungalows.

They run their fingers over
the rucks and valleys of pure new wool,
weigh up the pros and cons of underlay.

I can hear the words fall from his lips
as I make tea in the staff room,
'Silver Sage, Soapstone, Muslin'.

He whispers in my ear at night
when the children are asleep.
'Sultana, Prairie, Pollen,
Fleece, Linseed, Cinnabar'.

Our congruent bodies lie parallel,
an owl calls from the coppice,
he holds me firm like gripper rod.

My moans spill from the bed,
upholster the bare stone floor.

Mr Pepys's Inclination

If ever there was a euphemism, I was it.
He spotted me at St Olave's, mouthing
hymns to the booming organ.
Come back for wine and cake, he says,
his wife not cold, the sculptor
still chiseling her conversational mouth.

Seething Lane was steeped in learning.
He tried with me, took me to see
stocking weaving, the gilding of letters
used for print. But he soon
slid back to his friends.
I didn't mind not being married—

I had my maid, my bank account.
I liked to go about with him,
my hand resting on his dripping sleeve.
Who cares what powdered heads might think?
That Michaelmas those three armed men
held up our coach was warm beyond belief.

They poked the barrel at our driver's heart.
My moneybag pressed against my thigh,
I held my solid breath.
Sam gave up his silver rule, his gold pencil,
his magnifying glass. I sat tight,
willing my face to turn zinc white.

I didn't breathe a sigh till we got home.
Now I wear my diamond mourning ring,
I have two full presses of my own,
I keep his portrait on my wall,
beside the one of me, called Mrs Pepys.
That's me, in name, and history.

Around Thaxted

What am I to think now the trees
gesture with burnt orange,
a pheasant inhabits the middle of the road,
pyracanthas berries herald a corner?

That there is a script but not the time?
There is a script but not a place?

The wheels of my car avoid a dead rabbit,
the sky hovers between sugar pink and baby blue.

Your words drive the engine.
'In all conscience.' 'Tantalize.' 'Streatham.'
They navigate the bends.
'No point beating about the bush.'
They indicate the way.
'I'll think of you as I head on,
'I'll think of you as I head out.'

At the party sparks from a roman candle
light up the greenhouse,
a cockatoo shower squalls across the sky,
the massive Catherine wheel spins to magenta.
The back of everyone's head is you.

On the way home a deer lies by the road,
its antlers lean deep into the ditch.

Alcyone

I pushed my lips into his, to delay him,
he cupped my waist,
stroked my hot wet cheek.
I knew my father couldn't halt the winds
as a favour to my husband,
the blasts would rush from the cave as always,

to whip around his swilling ship.
My fear for Ceyx puckered my heart.
Refusing to heed my pleas
he promised to return
in two cycles of the moon—
as though his fate

rested on his own behest.
At the shore I waved,
till I could still see his mouth,
till I could still see his stature,
till his figure faded on the stern.
And still I stood, as sails

dissolved in violet mist.
I wept in our bed,
reached out for his warmth,
my tears turned cold
as they spread through the sheets.
I sewed a shirt for his return,

prayed each day for his love
to be safe in mine,
counted out the days
in dried gardenia leaves.
That night I dreamt of him
was filled with a thrill of stars.

He stood before me, naked,
his skin white as an egret's wing,
his hair and beard wet from the waves.
He told me of a storm—
how the wind had ripped
the width of the sails,

how the seams of the ship
tore easily, like new bread,
how the timbers sank beneath the sea
like stones dropped in a wishing pool.
He bid me mourn for him,
that he might not dwindle

in the desert of Hell unwept.
A knife cut a gulch
from my shoulder to my hip.
We should have died together.
Returning to the shore,
I scanned the greedy sea,

remembered his goodbye eyes,
his hands unthreading thick brown rope.
A face broke the surface,
floated closer, arms outstretched—
my husband's tender torso,
my husband's trusted hair.

'You come back to me like this?'
The sea welcomed my dive,
numbed my skin to a pelt.
I willed the water—'Soak my lungs,
fill the rift between my first sight of Ceyx
beneath a flowering almond tree, and this.'

He'd left me lonely as a planet.
Instead, I grew two wings,
my mouth lengthened to a beak,
I sped towards the sky where sun and moon
glinted on my cyan back.
Along a familiar creek, at lowest tide,

just as the light was giving out,
Ceyx joined me, his wings a mirror of mine.
We scalloped and skimmed the water's edge,
chikeeing to the coots.
Each winter, either side the solstice,
I lay my eggs at sea.

A Memory of Snow
for Esther

That night the gale tilted the foreshore,
    wide rain spat at the hills,
        you turned in your thin deep bed,
            asleep with staring eyes.

          As snow rose up the mountains,
      scree on peaks washed through,
   you dreamt of herons on goatherds,
of the way a buzzard flew.

You woke to six bare mountains,
    to one with a memory of snow,
        to sheep climbing the staircase,
            to blink at a face they know.

          A stag came into the garden,
      he bowed his head to the ground,
   dislodged his rack of antlers—
his gift for you to find.

'The Whole of the Rain in Every Month'
Richard Towneley's weather records 1677–1703, Towneley Hall, Burnley

Whether it's misling veils
or bucketing pounds
I certainly want to know.

Three times a day I pace the roof,
check the cylinder
nestling beneath the battlements.

I stare at the meniscus,
watching the passage of clouds,
choose my words with care—

'rain with hail', 'frost and fair',
'chequered and clear'.
I feel for the direction of the wind,

measure the weight of air.
My ribbed lists slide neatly
into olive wood drawers.

Along at Sheddon Clough
a ridge rests on a shelf of mist,
a bank of cloud blots a spur,

wind bustles through a cripple hole.
The same rain I collect
rushes down the veins of goits

and gathers up in storage ponds.
Released, it races at clods of clay,
hushing pebbles from high-prized lime.

Beside purging flax and sphagnum moss,
heaps of stones in rounded hills
colonize my rich ravine.

Figure

When I arrived Suilven
wore a scarf of cloud

across her shoulder.
Next day, pouting at Canisp,

a chestnut beret at half cock.
Her skirts were low

with mist on Thursday.
Today, her shape,

with sun, is kissed.

Climbing to the Kirkaig Falls

Before we part the treacle river runs beside,
the way is stippled, ochre leaves of silver birch,
a spring hangs down a russet cliff.

Climbing higher, major characters appear—
sleeping Suilven, Cul Beag, Cul Mor.

Behind, a V of sea slots in the sky,
thunder from the falls draws me on.

They are enough—
the whorls around intruding rocks,
the white barrage stained with peat.

Then a ravine opens
on the brightest butter yellow crown of leaves,
a heron streaks his grace along the valley to the shore.

The Second Drive to Dundonnell

was darker than the first,
shale surfaced from the mountainside,

the cog-sharp ridge jabbed
at soft blue light.

That time between the darkness and the day
when spaces stretch,

a misty film filters near from far,
sheep begin to think the road their own.

When water creaks with weight of rock,
land fuses sea with sky,

boats don't expect to move again.

River Torridge

I knew the river hid
behind the bank,
lying, like a length of silk,
stretched between the willows.

The surface ripped,
something dived—
gone too long to be a bird.

Weasel head above the water,
down he went again,
a flash of oily fur.

He swam up beside,
this time he stayed,
looking at me straight.
I walked to keep his pace.

I loved his length—
his tail his body,
his body his tail,
his tail the river's length.
We moved together
through the wind,
along the river's course.

Another dive,
I skimmed the current,
searching for his guise.

He'd gone on alone.
I felt him though,
gliding through
the river's strength.

Cloth

We stood, like stacks of bobbins
bursting over the road,
the Ogden River bubbled,

simmering over awkward stones,
the scarred hills leaned into Middle Mill.

Four hundred cheers helped
split the cleaved door.
We swarmed.

Men smashed cast iron frames,
slashed leather driving belts,
mashed beams, buckled yells.

Women snapped shuttles, reeds,
ripped the rippling yarns.

We yanked the power from the maw
of those machines as they'd
grabbed the food from ours.

I'd woven the worsted of the dress
I wore that day myself,
a chill still fed the April air.

Back on the cobbles again,
shouting for our men

I felt a tug behind, heard a scissor clip.
Loyal Holt hid his hand—
a piece of cloth from my skirt for proof.

LANCASTER CASTLE

For slats of the day I let my mind
bend beyond these prison walls,

to the day I married beneath a blood red arch,
my husband's face held in a hurried smile,
the ochre light glazing his hazel hair,

to the day dear Elizabeth screamed at the font.
I trailed her fingers over shapes around the bowl—

heart, goat, a pair of clutching sheers.
The cold stone calmed her for a while.
I will not think of Abraham or Robert—

their palms grew no wider than a leaf.
The hills are their fathers,

the scorching grass reaches over them in summer,
crisp with frost by November dusks.
No, I will not think of them.

My arms harbour memories of throwing the shuttle,
whipping it through the weft,

they flinch for want of warp and yell.
My feet flex, searching for wooden peddles,
to pull the pulleys, raise a shed.

My hair is frayed, my curls are gone,
I'm bald as a loom without a thread.

Sleeping Room

Should I think myself lucky
when the candles go out at nine?
The sour stink of sweat can't get much worse,
there's boiled beef, herring, cheese,
more than I'd ever see at Pleasant Street.
Antimony and nitrates ease my lungs.
And I'm to live.

I'll not see the Drop Room now,
feel the rope smooth around my throat.
I'm to be made an example,
with my manufacturing husband,
his churchwarden father.
Death has been exchanged,
I'm to be flung to a foreign country
for life, if a life would be its name.

What I want is my husband's shoulder,
my hand sliding round his cheek,
his mouth finding mine,
the heat of our bodies confounding
the cool night air.
Instead I'm in this vicious sleeping room,
dank and dark as a vixen's lair.

She-lag number 32

Two days fettered to the outside of a stagecoach,
irons pounding my wrists and ankles,

my bones near shook themselves free of their joints.
When I thought I could no longer stand it

I pushed one scene into my mind—
George and Elizabeth hurtling

towards my arms as the turnkey looked on,
peering into their slate blue eyes,

forcing down my chest pain,
gathering up their velvet words.

I knew them then as I never would again.

I huddle below deck on this dripping ship,
the Harmony, she-lag number 32,

waiting for our quota of skinners,
till-friskers, murders, perjurers.

I stroke my arm, remember the down
on Elizabeth's skin.

LETTER TO MY HUSBAND, 12 NOVEMBER 1827, SYDNEY

I hope these few lines find you well.
For three weeks of the five month voyage
I lay in a hospital bed.
I'm healthy now, Thank God.

My master is kind but his family is large,
six children to wash for,
sewing and nursing, one child in arms.
Each day longer than a month.

I hope my daughter is took good care of,
I am thinking of her often.
We have no liberty. Stay out late or stray
and we are pushed in the Watchhouse.

Or sent to the women's factory for punishment.
Please give my kind love
to my mother, your father and mother,
my brothers and sisters, all enquiring friends.

Sydney is a very fine town, a deal of building going on.
Will my sentence be mitigated?
I should die of despair if I thought
you could not get something done.

Please give my respects to Mr Hurst, Mr Turner.
You talk of coming to New South Wales,
there is none of your trade here.
In fact no manufacturing at all.

Butter and eggs are very dear, poultry dear in general.
I hope and trust that none I know
will share this fate with me.
You must answer this letter quickly,

I shall be anxious to hear from you.
Send all particulars of my little girl.
Please pay the postage when you write.
Eighteen thousand miles is the distance I am from you.

PARRAMATTA RIVER, AUGUST

I could keep on absconding, crawling
through the ridged hole in the outside wall,

could keep on being caught,
confined to cell, fed on bread and water,

wearing the cold weight of spiked iron around
my waning neck. Or I could

slide my foot inside this river, slip slowly
down the sandy bank, drop

like a stone beneath the silky surface. Have done.
Yearning ploughs me up, its

blade cuts me to the bone. This way
I'd find some peace. God may forgive me.

I want to feel the water creep up my thighs,
my belly, my aching arms. I want

its presence on my lips, filling my ears,
smoothing my stifled hair.

Come. Push yourself forward. Let
the river fill you up, let it make a statue

in its waves, holding my image in its depths
for the rest of this worn out winter.

Queen of the Night

Have you any idea how thick the dark can be?
A torch burns only as bright as a candle,
a candle is a breadcrumb in the dust.

The moon spends its days here,
the sun its nights. Neither can lift the faces
of the stillborn children at my side.

As Lady of the Great Place I barter the living
for the living, decide who stays to drink stale water,
who goes to veil the world as wraiths.

When I think night has come
I rest my talons in the pool,
close my eyes to see —

tawny streams running through a calcite jar,
a bend of light caught on a column,
the orange rush through carnelian beads.

Before I sleep I picture the sky, lapis lazuli,
reflected in water channels,
making mosaic between two rivers —

the swift Tigris rising in the east,
languid Euphrates falling to the west.
Day and night both cut this fragile land with balm.

Death

She stands behind me, pokes my shoulder.
I turn, she looks away.
She brings wet logs for my fire.

She has three mice—
one drops beneath the crockery
into the washing up water,
the second gets trapped in the waste bin,
the third hurries into the humane trap
stored in the lean-to drawer
and lies unnoticed for several days.

She can do the tango and the twist.
Her fuchsia lipstick is smudged
all over her chin.

Triptolemus

My limbs burn now as they did then
when Demeter placed me on the fire.
She sought to scorch

mortality from my infant core.
Pain began to find its end,
I felt eternal life teasing at my grasp.

Whose mother would not scream at such a sight?
She showed her doubt, her faith curled up,
Demeter took her easy gift and left.

So here I lie, my face lined
like gullies down a mountainside,
my children lined beside my bed.

Would I have wanted more?
I thread these moments on a golden string—
my daughters dancing in yellow fields

their hair a shimmer above the corn,
my wife tracing emerald hills above our home,
the first warmth of the year stinging my cheek.

Too many moments would dilute their grip,
I'd learn to hide from early season sun,
I'd see my daughters failing one by one.

Though now a thousand daggers pierce my skin
I die as I have lived,
with night and streaming day within.

NYNY

Beware,
I
have
New York
in my eyes.
Balconies with a
closed lid of snow,
two poached eggs in
a cup, the flash of
static as my finger
hits the Chrysler tower.
A lift flying eighty
floors in less than
a minute, a lift
which never comes,
an unflushable toilet,
a toilet which
flushes when I open
the door. A window
from my room looks
into an opposite room—
a woman wears
antennae to watch
TV. A tall man with
wide Halloween hair,
black lenses in his
eyes, bends low to
kiss his small pale
girlfriend on the
forehead. The snow
is stacked in mountain
ranges at the end of
each sidewalk.
Care is needed to get
across to the other side.

Dinner in the Iguanodon Mould

You have to be careful with the yolk,
make sure it doesn't muddy the white,
you want stiff peaks and I have to say
mine were splendid from the first.

Buisson de Meringue, a thicket of the stuff,
aux Confiteur, standing on the table
next to jellies, nougat, Charlotte de Russe.

Though how those gents
had room I'll never know;
after Mock Turtle soup, no end of fish,
removes, choice of entrées,
then pheasant, woodcock, snipe.

I only saw one hand reach out
for pines and filberts at the end.

We listened to the speeches out behind the tent.
I stroked the neck of the plesiosaurus,
stuffed as he was with bricks and tiles.

There was praise for the pioneers
of this new science of palaeontology,
the names were read from banners overhead:
Mantell, Buckland, Cuyier, Owen.

I could only think of little Mary Anning
collecting fossils down in Lyme,
struck by lightening, dying young,
selling seashells by the shore—

how she deserved a banner.

I make new things from ingredients,
transforming flour into cake.
She dug at what's already there,
found skeletons in the dust

with every bone joined to another
just as when they were alive.

Lifeline

Your clothes still smell of cinnamon and garlic,
your hand of lavender and musk,
despite the drenching and the soaking,

the days you must have floated
between stern and sodden deck.

Chesil's arm of pebbles beckoned,
guided you to Wyke,
and here you lie, who are you

with stained glass blue all round you
bringing your dead eyes alight?

You've knotted wrack and thongweed
plaited through your hair,
I'll pick it out and keep it,

lay these lilies at your feet,
bring flowers to you daily,
be your daughter while you need me,

sweep the aisle, wipe the altar,
I'll see you claimed, all right.

Your lips are grey as lias, your fingers
hold the air, your bones are made from beauty,
when I touch your arm, you care.

Breakdown

I've lost the use of the comma,
M's are gone from my finger ends
along with N, V, and Z.

Correspondents enjoy Sodoku emails,
they say they like the early morning workout—
guessing what the dashes mean.

But I must phone India to replace my password,
choosing one which skirts the broken keys.

Kisses are difficult
without the cross-hatch of an X.

The Poets' Strike

Elastic bands are strapped round notebooks,
imaginative thought herded down a cul de sac,
the absence of metaphor, withdrawn from
news bulletins, is mourned around the world.

There's a dull ache on the tube,
a child is admonished for skipping a rhyme,
daffodil bulbs grow blind of blooms.

At eleven o'clock a shiver runs through
the inhabitants of all towns beginning with S,
the mouths of librarians are down turned,
larks drop with shock from the sky.

Stitched People
after Louise Bourgeois' fabric figures

The stitched people are
pink beyond redemption,
their knees are split,
their stuffing overflows
like water from a weir.
They have water on the knee.

Quilted, criss-crossed skin,
so many scars,
each segment holding in
a section of intestine,
a quadrant of liver,
a ventricle of the heart.

Pinned to each, a memory—
eating the address of a boy
who rattled railings,
jumping from a ten foot wall
to catch a falling love,
drooling at Matisse
            reclining nudes
on a childhood bed.

I'm hanging by a thread.
Push the needle in again.

I Slipped from the Womb Fully Clothed

I slipped from the womb fully clothed,
make-up in tact, ready for the long commute.

I touched the naked arms
of women descending ribs of escalators.
Eye contact was never enough.

One sombre Tuesday at London Bridge
I somersaulted down the platform
along the custard yellow line.

The guard sympathized,
his were the only words I could hear,
'Let the passengers . . . let the passengers . . .'

Inside the carriage I stared at faces.
Who could be my friend?
Who had I known in another life?

A woman talked non-stop to Bank as if to me.
I was her fellow student,
marvelling at her teacher

and the improbable arrival of stringed instruments.
Tomorrow we would practise a sonata
at long shuttered windows.

Returning, I rested my head on my neighbour's shoulder
and dared to close my eyes.
He let me sleep.

I dreamt I was a Cyclops, shooting bolts of thunder
the length of the Northern Line.

Herbal Source
A list on a pavement sign outside a shop selling Chinese medicine

WEIGHT LOSS

When I lost half my body weight I was beyond recognition.
I'd flow down the high street with heels
and bare knees, gleaming a smile.
I felt nearer the sky.
It was easier not to explain,
to simply walk on by an acquaintance
who looked straight through me.
Half of me had disappeared;
the other half could take up gambling,
lie in bed till midday, buy cashmere in the spring.
Instead, I walked into another house and became a second
     wife.
A child hugged his knees in the corner of the sofa,
a brown sunflower climbed above the chimney stack.

HAY FEVER

On days of pollen rise flashes of light highlight the city—
tiers of windows closed against the grains.
My washing line lies bare.
The stocks I would have cut stay with their soil.
Water from a second shower runs in tributaries
down my legs and away to the breezy sea.

Hair Loss

My follicles are resting,
easing their way into shedding my hair.
I find sheaves on my pillow,
down the back of a chair,
they float down my bathwater like reeds.
Soon there will be nothing to stroke,
save the head of my babe,
as her silken down lengthens
past the nape of her neck.

Anxiety

A lark hovers in my chest,
sild slip through my veins,
my hip bones are egg cases born of whelks.
A piccolo plays a note which doesn't stop,
my feet keep sinking into sand.
I long for a walnut surface to lie on,
for a willow tree to surround me,
for a parent with a gentle hand.

STRESS

My father has another life.
He'd wake me in the morning,
push his whiskers to my cheek,
spread toast, clatter cutlery,
wave from the shining door.
I'd hear footsteps in the evening,
his key turning in the lock.
My father has another life.
Both ends of the day
belong to someone else.

MENOPAUSE

I know she'll come back but it's the evidence I miss,
her 'product' in the bathroom,
her washing folded on the stairs,
velvet cushions imprinted with her limbs.
I stand in her room and name the animals—
seal, bear, badger, dolphin, monkey, whelp.
There are eight strands of hair in her hairbrush.
I tease them out, thread them round my fingers,
then push them back amongst the stubble of the bristles.

SEX DRIVE PROBLEM

Not so much a problem as a mismatch.
I'm like the Minotaur's father,
ready to bolt from the edge of a field.
She's satisfied with her orchids,
delicacy and grace, delicacy and grace.
When my blood's up I want
to rent the air with her screams,
fold into her like high surf
cascading to join the shore.

INFERTILITY

My womb is filled with baby grows,
with smudged grey photos of globular fingers
and a rounded brow.
There's a Silver Cross pram with a hood,
a ring of pastel teething rings,
cloth books arranged on melamine shelves, easy to clean.
The walls are covered in a story—
a daughter loved her father more than fresh meat loves salt.

Optometrist

Leaning towards your vitreous humour
I'm closer to you than your lover,
my breath at odds with your rhythm,
quiet as an autumn breeze.

Through my lens I can see the shape
of your dreams, the texture of your past,
how far your blind spot
                              blights your life.

There's a scene playing out with a tired old man,
he holds your hands while you weep,
his words are fished
                              from parallel streams.

And now there's a pool of fresh water,
with a bracelet of flat grey stones
where you dangle your feet for an afternoon
then pick a path
                              through a maze.

My hands make the shape of your eye,
on paper I reveal your vision—
the sphere and axis of your tender sight,

your tendency, when cornered,
to avoid the cadences
                              of light.

The Registrar

She writes in pale blue indelible
across the ruled page—

place of birth, cause of death.
In time, the ink will darken to slate.

Later still, the veins of her letters
will fill with indigo.

My father's blood drained from his face
to gather at his spine.

His chilly skin, still smooth and soft
was what I recognized.

She writes with care, her vowels round,
'Ischaemic Heart Disease'.

Through her blouse
are flicks of lace.

Her pumping heart is near.

Rock

You would liked to have seen the kestrel,
taut in a dark cavern,
keeping watch from his vantage point.
I know I can find him again.

The rock dropped black and sheer
from his hooded platform,
slabs stacked hard against each other
to the ragged moor below.

Beside, a soft round hill, a spoil heap,
workings piled beneath
grass grows on what's left behind
when quarried rock is spent.

We walked these hills,
I came to you, the main thing was to leave.
It's returning now that spurs my life,
the sight of birches, dried brown leaves,

staggering down the slope.
An envelope of milky light
flitting through the weighted sky.

Late September

As I puzzled at the succulent
missing from my parents' grave

he stood, hands clasped,
his prayers a murmur over lower slopes.

Two adjacent graves, tilled earth piled high,
eight vases sunk up to their waists.

Arranging roses, hybrid tea,
he held a conversation with his mother,

then another with his wife.
Finally, the housework—

one by one he picked up leaves
beside each grave,

held them in a bucket to be safe.

It was late September,
there were many leaves to come.

Pyjama Walk

for Warren

She looped the cord back into a bow
and tugged at the blue striped jacket.

Through puddles her painted toenails
glowed like closed anemones.

Her feet felt the planes of stones,
her face the chill of a northern wind.

Passing by, an elderly woman
in a nightie wished her 'Happy Christmas'.

Away in the distance, sunlight glinted
on a writhing lake,

a rack of hills faded to rippling blue.
Standing on the hillside stared at by rams,

glanced at by ponies,
the months of the following year clothed her,

in a jumper knitted with nests,
a scarf woven with dry stone walls,

and a blanket of gates
opening down to her ankles.

Crab Apples

The crab apples you flung at me
stung my cheeks like splashes of milk
from a scalding pan.

You were jubilant in your aim,
stalking the garden's top path
with a steely smile.

Inside, you'd hide in your room,
your foot against the door,
a halo of beer mats

balanced on the picture rail.
Sooner or later I'd notice
my flamenco dancer missing

from the chest of drawers,
the matador left behind with couples
from Peru, Amsterdam, Budapest.

Your shoulder heaved against mine,
the stubborn door thinning between.
Now we must polish our parents' home,

sweep fallen moss from flags,
disperse the chest of drawers.
We must ready this home

for strangers,
who will walk between rooms
as sunlight silhouettes new shoots

of honeysuckle through amber leaves,
they will linger over the peach flush
of a bullfinch in the copper beech.

We must hand over this home
like a garland bestowed by a luminary
on a talented, teeming child.

Pinnacles

The placemats slip from her hands
replaced by sweet peas —
ripples of pink and mauve,
cream pockets holding sweet scent
she cannot smell.

Knives refuse to line up on the table,
instead a steady wren hops
between salt bowl and pepper stack.

Sturdy amaryllis stand on the patio
easing into August sun.
Next year their blooms will be
gigantic with red.

Kitchen roll triumphs as napkins,
buds of dried lavender froth from bowls,
her winged hands leaf through loved books
for a relevant quote —
Portia, pertinent for the credit crunch.

And all the while we marvel
at the extent of her smiles,
the brio in her eyes,
the pinnacles of her journeys
as she inches from room to room.

Colchicums

Their buttery noses slide through the ground,
leafless, naked, like a newborn
                              braving the wind.

At full height their mauve transparency
flickers
          across the flower beds
spreading like thin waves
                              on a foreshore.

Those done with living lie across the ground,
nudged by nubs of shoots gathering strength

to stretch towards
                    the spawning skies.

Antica Locanda Montin

I'm left with one set of clothes
hanging in the wardrobe,

the bells still thrill the skies,
swallows mill between roofs.

There are blank masks to be wrapped,
postcards to be planted in guidebooks,

black pasta to pack between shirts.
Then, this room, dismantled

of its playing cards and torches,
will no longer hold the papier-mâché

layers of our days, the binding waking
and sleeping, the caul of our conversation,

the woven skein of our ways.

Notes

'CHORISTER, ST SAVIOUR'S CHURCH, SOUTHWARK, 1607', p. 13.

Edmund Shakespeare, William's youngest actor brother, died aged 27 and is buried in St Saviour's Church—now Southwark Cathedral.

'MR PEPYS'S INCLINATION', p. 17.

Mary Skinner was Samuel Pepys's mistress for 33 years. His contemporaries referred to her as 'Mr Pepys's inclination'.

'ALCONE', p. 19.

A kingfisher is also known as a halcyon.

'THE WHOLE OF THE RAIN IN EVERY MONTH', p. 23.

Richard Towneley, of Towneley Hall Burnley, became the first weatherman in England when he began to make systematic measurements of rainfall using a gauge he designed himself.

'LANCASTER CASTLE', p. 29.

A yell is a heddle or heald—the looped wires through which the warp yarn is threaded on a loom.

A shed is the area between the upper and lower warp yarns through which the shuttle passes to weave the weft.

'SHE-LAG NUMBER 32', p. 31.

A skinner was a woman who enticed children to go with her then stripped them of their clothes; or, as a prostitute, stripped drunken customers and sold their clothes.

'PARRAMATTA RIVER, AUGUST', p. 34.

Mary Hindle was born in Haslingden, East Lancashire in 1799. After the machine breakers riots of 1826 she was probably one of the first female political prisoners to be transported to Australia. She ran away twice from the Parramatta Female Factory in New South Wales and took her own life on 21st August 1841, aged 42.

'DINNER IN THE IGUANODON MOULD', p. 39.

On New Year's Eve 1853 Benjamin Waterhouse Hawkins held a seven course dinner for 21 guests in the belly of a model dinosaur to celebrate his 33 life-sized sculptures of prehistoric monsters in Crystal Palace Park. The catering was undertaken by the Anerley Tavern.

'LIFELINE', p. 41.

Mary Anning (paleontologist and fossil hunter) visited the body of a woman washed ashore in 1815 after the Alexander sailing ship was wrecked off the Dorset coast.